MW01146316

Kake King, LLC
info@kakeking.com
www.kakeking.com

Dedication

This book is dedicated to Me. So many years I've struggled with finishing this or not thinking I was good enough. Self- doubt caused so much internal pain for me. I release all of that negative energy and replace it with positive vibes!

I would also like to dedicate this to everyone who has believed in me, supported me, and pushed me towards my purpose.

Lastly, to my family, & all of my besties, I love you!

We made it!!!!

Jeromie "Kake King" Jones
www.kakeking.com

Foreword

When I think of success in the baking industry, I know that it takes a combination of creativity and innovation. That's why I am honored to write this foreword for my colleague and friend, Jeromie Jones, who is one of the most innovative people I know!

From his time as a home baker in Mississippi to his massive success in the e-commerce space, Jeromie is constantly reinventing himself showing hope and positivity to his fans and followers.

His charismatic personality and infectious humor have touched people all over the world and I'm excited that he has written this book to bring even more of his knowledge, expertise, insight to inspire the baking community.

Porsha Kimble | YCD
www.yourcakediva.com

Disclaimer

One important thing to remember is that this book is written from my personal experience with opening my bakery. Everyone's experience will be different,

you may have it completely easy and the entire bakery opening process is a breeze! Every city, every landlord, every space, every health inspector, will all be different.

Every effort has been made to accurately represent this product and its potential and there is no guarantee that you will earn any money using these techniques. No content contained in this book shall be construed as formal business or legal advice.

Introduction

Thank you for purchasing my new eBook! You either purchased this book because you are playing with the idea of opening a bakery or you want to educate yourself just in case you one day get to that point. Either way, I applaud you for taking the step to educate yourself more about the topic. I wrote this book to answer the many questions that home bakers have about one day opening their own bakery. The majority of the cake and treat community dream to one day open their own storefront, but the idea can be scary and overwhelming. There are not many resources out there to help aid in this un-denying fear. The main problem that many home bakers face is, there are not many people who have crossed that bridge that you can easily reach out and talk to who won't bite your head off! Luckily, I don't mind pouring out my experiences with it to help others! Now, no two situations will be the same, but it's my hope that my experience can help you!

I have been a self-taught cake artist for 14 years now. I normally tell people, even though I'm not formally trained in a more structured culinary environment, I did however attend YouTube academy where I earned my PhD! No amount of formal training can teach substitute experience and experience has been my greatest teacher.

I am also a two-time Food Network competitor on *Cake Wars* and The *Food Network Challenge*. I have competed in many cake competitions and come out with even more knowledge that helped me to become a better artist. I found that I like many people, I learn best through hands-on, applied knowledge, so I decided to start taking hands- on classes with some pretty amazing cake artists to further my skills.

"If you truly want it bad enough, you will stick it out and see it through"

I hope that this book guides you into a better understanding of what really happens behind the scenes when trying to open a brick-and-mortar bakery. Listen, it's not easy! You will be frustrated.

You will want to give up. You will doubt yourself. You will drain your bank account. You will even want to walk away. However, if you truly want it bad enough, you will stick it out and see it through. As the saying goes, nothing worth having will ever come easy!

What's Your Why?

Now ask yourself: Why do you want to open a bakery? Is it because you've outgrown your kitchen or home studio? Do you feel like it will force people to take your business more seriously? Whatever your reason, I urge you to make the decision after you have done all the research and educated yourself. Opening any type of business can be expensive and involves a lot of hard work. Are you ready for the commitment it will take? Let me take you through the journey I encountered for what I call the birth of my bakery.

Chapter 1: The Dream

I never envisioned opening a bakery, nor did I have any idea I would ever be doing cakes professionally! I grew up with so many creative ideas of what my life would be like.

After graduating high school, I went to cosmetology school. My dream was to become a platform stylist for

Paul Mitchell. I wanted to travel around the world as a master colorist and cut stylist. Like many dreams, that wasn't my reality. I realized I'd probably never make it out of my small hometown doing hair for a living in Mississippi. I decided to go to college.

I went onto college and literally did hair nearly every day out of my dorm room. While in college, I fell head over heels in love with a guy. I decided to move out of my dorm on campus and into his apartment. This was my first time really ever being in love in my adult life.

Things really went downhill the deeper we got into the relationship. This was my first experience with depression. Things somehow got so bad that I attempted to commit suicide. Here I was in my early twenties, ready to end it all. After spending almost a week in a treatment center for depression, I made up in my mind about what I needed to do.

I worked my butt off to get my own place. No one really knew what was going on besides my fraternity line brothers and my cousin who truly became my saving grace. I reached out to her and told her what was going on and she wasted no time sending me the deposit for my first apartment! One morning, I waited until he left for work and I literally packed up everything I had and moved into my new apartment. I had no idea what it would be like to be on my own but somehow, I kept trusting God even in the midst of my heartache. I didn't have a real plan when I moved out, I just knew I needed to be in my own space and away from that toxic environment.

" I kept trusting God even in the midst of my heartache."

After a few months, I guess my friends got tired of me moping around. A good friend of mine was visiting me for the weekend and told me that I needed to do something to get my mind off of the past.

We were walking through Wal-Mart and ended up in the cake decorating aisle. He picked up a kit and told me, "Since you like cooking so much, why don't you try baking." I looked at him like he was stupid, but I didn't object. I took the kit home, and it sat on my counter for about a week.

I started watching YouTube videos about cake decorating and quickly became obsessed. I would literally be in class watching videos instead of paying attention to the lecture. I found myself becoming really interested in baking and the art of decorating. I finally decided to give it a try and let's just say my enthusiasm was short-lived by the reality that I wasn't really that good at it!

I studied book after book and recipe after recipe. I had a part-time job at a book store so most of my breaks were spent looking through cake books and magazines trying to figure out recipes. I started working on perfecting my baking skills and really took an interest in the science of baking. I knew early only that I was not a fan of scratch -made cakes! No matter how many recipes I tried, I just didn't like the taste and texture of them. There were so many factors that went into making sure they came out right!

I still remember my first cake! It was awful!!!!! The taste was gritty, flavorless, and the design was just God awful!!! But I didn't give up!! I look back on my past work now and think, wow what was I thinking when I did that?! I had to really work to even be considered 'good'. I started researching cake groups

on Facebook and learned that there was a whole world out there of people who loved cake just as much as I was starting to.

I began researching and studying design styles and techniques. Essentially, I went backward in the beginning. I was so focused on learning trends that I skipped over learning basic baking fundamentals. I worked on fondant for a while until I felt I had pretty much gotten it down pat. During that time, fondant cakes were a big hit and seemed to be very expensive from what I had seen. I began trying to perfect the small things in my work. Borders and roses were almost the death of me. No matter how much I practiced, they always sucked! I found out that the craft store in my area held cake decorating classes. I signed up and started going a few nights a week. I made it all the way through all of the courses, and you couldn't tell me I wasn't the shit then! I still had work to do though.

I eventually moved to a new city and started taking the gift I had more seriously. It's funny how people have more faith in our abilities than we do in ourselves. I was approached by a customer to do her daughter's birthday party and this was the first big cake order that I'd ever had! I had never done a large tier cake before and I was damn near terrified, but I had already taken this woman's money, so I had to do it. The worst part was that the party was damn near 2.5 hours away from where I lived!

"I started posting my cakes on social media and I quickly developed a following. People were asking me to create cakes left and right for different events and milestones."

I studied day in and day out on how I would achieve the look and somehow, I pulled the whole thing together! To this day the lady still brags on how great of a job I did, and I still say it looked a hot ass mess! I started posting my cakes on social media and I quickly developed a following. People were asking me to create cakes left and right for different events and milestones.

Becoming a Professional

That was the beginning of what I would say is my professional cake career. As I began to get more serious about my work, my interest level also grew with wanting to make sure I was branding myself correctly. I never really gave my hobby a name, it wasn't really a business then – or so I thought. I started researching ways to legalize everything and learned that I needed to obtain an LLC and come up with my business name. This really made me want to take my craft a little more seriously.

Even though I was working from home, I still wanted people to take me seriously when ordering. I finally came up with the name *JustKaking Custom Cakes &*

Treats. I wanted something catchy, so I changed the C in cake to a K.

Now that I had a name it was then time to obtain my LLC to register my name and business with the state. This process was actually fairly simple. LLC is short for Limited Liability Company. Basically, the LLC separates your personal money from the business. In the event you should ever be sued, the customer would go after your business in which falls under the LLC and not your personal assets.

An LLC can be obtained by visiting the website of the Secretary or Department of State's office in your state. The website will vary from state to state, but somewhere on the site, you will see the section to formulate a new business. Once you've done that, you now have your business registered with the state! Every year, you will need to also file an annual report outlining how your business did for the year or reporting period (this will also vary from state to state).

Figuring out which business structure is right for your bakery can be confusing. I created a simple chart explaining the basics of each business structure type and when they might be the right choice. Keep in mind, this is just an *overview*!

Disclaimer: The information in this chart and in the expanded workbook version should in no way be taken as formal business or legal advice.

For a more detailed explanation of business structure types, download the printable *Home to Bakery Workbook*, which gives you a detailed breakdown, helpful resources, and note pages.

Piercing the Corporate Veil

It wouldn't be right for me to touch on business structures and their benefits without addressing something known as 'piercing the corporate veil.' What is it?

Well, one of the biggest benefits of forming an LLC or Corporation is the protection of your personal assets. However, what most people won't tell you is that, in some cases, your assets *are* indeed at risk if someone decides to sue your business. To put it simply, just filing the paperwork and paying the fee is NOT enough to keep your personal money safe.

When you set up your business, there are four things you need to make sure you do while running it to keep the corporate veil intact:

1) **Create formal procedures for your business:** In most states, you are required to file annual reports for

your business (for both LLCs and Corporations). Other formal

business procedures depend on your business structure type:

> *Corporations*: Form and updated bylaws regularly, issue stock to shareholders, hold initial and annual meetings for shareholders and directors, pay corporate taxes.

> *LLCs*: Create and regularly update a formal operating agreement, issue membership certificates (if there is more than one owner), record membership transfers, hold initial and annual member meetings.

Regardless of what type of business structure you choose, always check with your state's registering entity to find out *exactly* what is required.

2) **Document! Document! Document!**: if you make any decisions that will affect the business or hold meetings, it is

important to document these events. Keep electronic or physical copies of any contracts you company enters into and record meeting minutes during any initial or annual member meetings.

3) **Keep Business and Personal Assets Separate:** I can't stress this one enough! The owner(s)' assets **MUST** be kept separate from the company's assets. Open a business checking account and credit card using your IRS-issued Tax ID or EIN and make sure to use it only for business expenses. Also, avoid keeping personal property and business equipment together.

4) **Get Your Business Name Out There**: Creating invoices, marketing material, and business cards with your company's name and logo serves to broadcast that your business exists. In some states, you may be required to take

out a small ad in a local publication to announce your business. Any documents you sign should bear your company's name as well.

How do these four things relate to the corporate veil? Let's say your company is sued. The judge will likely order that your business dealings be investigated. If it is revealed that you did not follow one or more of these recommendations (for example, mixing your business and personal assets), the corporate veil is then considered 'pierced' and your personal assets may become up for grabs.

Do yourself a favor and don't just stop at registering your business. Make sure you do your research concerning what your state requires. While a lot of people form their LLC or Corporation without help, it's a good idea to talk to a professional who is knowledgeable about your state's requirements.

Chapter 2: A Hustle for The Hustle

Like I said before, a bakery was not in my plans. I was pretty content with working from home and seeing all the profit I brought in! At that time, I had no idea about pricing, cost of goods, overhead, etc. What I was an expert at was being a hustler! I had secured an awesome job with a major insurance company and was doing pretty well for myself to be so young, but I wanted more.

I came up with an idea to generate some quick cash and also get my name out there more in the city. It would take a lot of effort, but I knew that if it was a success, it would bring in a lot of money. Guess what, it worked! I decided that throughout the week I would allow people to place small orders for treats and have them pick them up on Sundays after church. At first, the idea seemed pretty small, I was bringing in about $500 profit. As word increased, I had to come up with a better strategy. This is when *Sweetsation Sunday* was birthed.

Creating My Business Strategy

As my name grew, I knew that my business strategy had to improve if I wanted to attract more customers. This is when I came up with a plan to improve sales and increase my visibility in the city. I did what some marketing analysts call market research. I will go into more detail about this in a later chapter.

Basically, I checked out what others were doing in my area and learned that I was literally the only person tapping into this market. The best thing about it was, I held this event on Sundays after church. I was able to create a market that no one else had thought of.

"As my name grew, I knew that my business strategy had to improve if I wanted to attract more customers. This is when I came up with a plan to improve sales and increase my visibility in the city."

We all know that after church, all black people are starving! I timed everything just right and set boundaries. So, let's back up to the planning stages. I knew that, for what I had in mind, I needed to be extremely organized because this could get very overwhelming really fast! I still had a full- time job, so I had to be smart about my plan. This is where I coined the phrase, **"You must have a hustle for the hustle!"**

I used my 9-to-5 job to do all of my work for my business. I even took advantage of the customers I had coming into my office. Any chance I got, I made sure I put my work in front of a customer. I came up with a text message ordering system, I would post my weekly menu on social media and customers would need to text me their order and I would put everyone's order on a spreadsheet to keep up with what I had to do. Here's an example of my weekly order chart:

Creating this chart was my lifesaver! This allowed me to keep up with everyone's order and the total

amount owed. This was during a time when you could actually trust that people would pick up the order they placed without sticking you with the products! I would start baking the items on Thursday evening and begin getting prepped for the weekend. This hustle quickly grew so big that the line on Sundays literally grew around the apartment complex I lived in! Cars would be lined up everywhere for pickup!

I learned things during this time that would later help me tremendously. One of the key lessons was strategizing and menu planning. It's impossible to go into anything without a plan of action. Many times, I see people who have great ideas in the community jump straight into things with no plan, no research, and most importantly no knowledge of the area they are going into. People want a quick way to get rich and that's not the case when it comes to the sweets

community! Menu planning was more than just posting a few flavors. I had to truly create flavors that would catch people's attention and draw them in with

the appearance of my social media postings! There are many programs out there to design your menu if you decide to do something like this. We get into that later in the planning chapter!

Over time, I began thinking, I just may be on to something. People were really enjoying the products that I was making. One day a light bulb went off and the thought arose about opening a bakery! I knew that at my age, a loan was out of the question, so I would have to be very strategic in my planning. I used *Sweetsation Sunday* as well as weekly cake orders as a way to save money. Eventually, the whole pre-order system became a full-time job, and I couldn't keep up with the demand. This is when the idea came to me of an in-house bakery on Sundays. So instead of taking pre-orders I would create a menu and bake hundreds of items. I would allow people to come in and choose the items they wanted and box them up just as you would when you walked into a bakery! This was genius!

"People want a quick way to get rich and that's not the case when it comes to the sweets community!"

Not only did the idea work, but I also literally sold out every Sunday! Each week my menu grew more and more as my skill level advanced, and I would add more items that weren't so basic. Cupcakes, cake pops, gourmet apples, and dipped strawberries were among my most popular items. I was raking in over $2000 in weekly sales!

I made a post one week that I wanted to challenge myself and see just how far I could go. I would see the show on Food Network, *Cupcake Wars,* and I kept saying I knew I could do what they were doing! So, I set a plan to have my biggest sale event to date and bake 1000 cupcakes! Not only did I meet my goal, but I actually exceeded it! I had never seen so much money being legally made in such a short amount of time!

I grew hungry for more and my hunger for opening my own bakery grew. But how could I do this? I had no idea how much it would even cost – building, equipment, supplies, employees – all these thoughts were constantly on my mind. I started doing more and more research on the idea and, the more I researched, the idea didn't seem so absurd. This was the beginning of my plan for my escape out of my boring everyday job and onto a path of entrepreneurship.

Chapter 3: Finding the Space

In the last chapter, I spoke about the importance of effectively planning and organizing your idea. I knew going in that opening a bakery was a huge project to undertake and I had no formal business knowledge. I knew that I had to do something about all the business I was generating at home.

Like many home bakers, the fear of getting caught by the health department for not having a legal space was looming over my head. There is one thing about people in the sweets community that will never change: jealousy! The crab mentality will always be a downfall of the community. As soon as your competition halfway across town sees that you are doing pretty good, that's when the hate starts! I dealt

with it on a major level. The harder I worked, the more it seemed people would work to tear down what I was building. I started to put my plan in place.

In my full-time job, there were days that I was required to go out into the field and visit various businesses to generate leads for potential quotes. This was the perfect time for me to start looking for prospective spaces. I would literally be all over the city viewing properties. One day while I was out, I stumbled upon a shopping complex that was right down the street from where I worked. There were many vacancies in the plaza, and it seemed to be in a pretty central location right off the highway.

"There is one thing about people in the sweets community that will never change: jealousy! The crab mentality will always be a downfall of the community."

I had passed by this plaza every day and never noticed the empty storefronts in it. I walked up to the empty space and looked through the window. It was a complete mess! It was once an old tanning salon so I instantly knew that getting it to a workable space would be impossible. Not to mention, it was a huge space so I knew it would be expensive to renovate!

When you're looking for potential spaces, it's important to keep in mind a few key deciding factors:

- LOCATION! LOCATION! LOCATION!

- Can the building be easily found?

- Are there any other businesses nearby that will create additional foot traffic?

- Is the space too large or too small for your needs?

- Is there adequate lighting in the parking lot in the event you are working late?

- Will the space require an extensive renovation?

- Is the space zoned for a bakery or food service establishment? You can get this information from city hall.

- Is the building structurally sound?

These are some of the questions I was posed with when I was looking for a potential space. I took a chance on the space anyway despite how it looked from the outside and reached out to the owner to take a look inside. We scheduled a time to meet later in the week. In the meantime, I started working through detail after detail in my head of how I could even pull this off financially. On the call, I forgot to even ask about the monthly rent!

"I had to envision myself in the space before I even had it."

I had my full-time job, and I was still saving the money I was making from cake orders and the weekly *Sweetsation Sunday* events. At the time, I had no idea that what I was about to embark upon would be one of my greatest accomplishments and the biggest head ever!

On the day I met with the owner about the space I did my initial walk-through and was overwhelmed at how huge the place was. There was plenty of space, as the building was over 2,000 square feet. I knew that I needed a space that would work for all of the avenues I wanted to take in my business.

I had to envision myself in the space before I even had it. I knew that I needed a retail area as I wanted to sell daily items. I also wanted enough space out front for a nice seating area for consultations or people who just wanted to drop in and enjoy their treats. The kitchen space needed to be big enough for possible classes and events as well as an office. This location had plenty of space for everything I wanted.

I finally asked the question I was dreading: How much? To my surprise, I was blown away at the owner's response. He said, "We can do $650 a month if you agree to sign a three-year lease." I looked at him in complete shock; $650 for a 2000 square foot building in a shopping plaza?! Too good to be true right? Well, guess what? It was!

I took a week to think things over and try to find someone who could even take on such a large project of renovating the place and do it for the budget I had. I knew I didn't want to go over $10,000 for everything and that even included equipment. This was my first mistake! I had no idea just how much renovations cost and all the things that go wrong when you are renovating a space.

An important question that I failed to ask the owner was how much of the renovation would they cover or if that was even possible. I learned later that they had, in fact, taken on the cost of another tenant's

renovations, and the tenant paid for the project in installments monthly! I have no idea why I didn't think about that then, but now I know it's because I

was uneducated in the world of negations and contracts. Had I negotiated this in the beginning I could have saved myself so much money and time!

As I told you earlier, the space used to be an old tanning salon, so it was so far from what I needed it to be. When you are choosing a space, it would be extremely helpful to take along someone that specializes in build-outs or renovations so they can give you an idea of what you're looking at. You may end up getting in way over your head before you even open your doors!

I finally signed on the space and agreed to the terms of the contract that I *assumed* I understood! Boy was I wrong! I agreed on a contractor that a friend referred to me who had a pretty good reputation for doing things like this. He assured me that the project really wasn't that extensive and that he could have it done in a few months. I was happy to hear this seeing that all of my money was going into this so I couldn't't pull back.

Before you begin tearing down anything, the city will require that you submit a drawing outlining where everything will be placed such as your furniture, equipment, sinks, etc. It is very important to create your vision of your space on this drawing. For me, this was where I had the opportunity to move things around that didn't make sense or add functionality to the space outside of what I had originally envisioned. The construction began and all of the existing interior was torn out to reveal a huge space that I could truly see myself in! This is when things got crazy!

The contractor had literally torn the place apart and taken it down to nothing but a brick building. He began getting very slow about completing tasks and meeting deadlines we had set. One of the major things was, he told me that he had acquired all the necessary permits with the city to begin work on the space, but this was so far from the truth! Part of his duties outlined in the contract included making sure all permits were in place and setting up the inspections. I was 25, I had no real idea what I was doing, so I assumed he knew this side of things. I was a baker, not a contractor!

Permits

So, let's pause. You have found your space and now

it's time to get legal! Here are a few things you will

need to obtain first. It is important to remember that

every state and city's requirements are different.

Some will require more paperwork, more permits,

more money spent, while others can be a cakewalk!

Don't get too bogged down and overwhelmed with

this, follow the steps that the city gives you and you

will be in compliance with their guidelines.

Permits are probably the most stressful part of

opening a bakery. There seemed to be a permit for

just about everything! There was even a permit

needed to put a sign on the building! Before you can begin tearing down any walls you will need to obtain a building permit or construction permit. Your contractor will need to outline a detailed plan of what construction will take place. There are also separate permits for certain jobs (electrical and plumbing work must be permitted separately). You must also acquire a food handler permit and pass a health department inspection.

Some of the key permits can be found below:

Business License

What it is: All legitimate business activities are regulated by a local, state, or federal agency and you need a valid business license if you want to operate legally.

Why you need it: You need a business license to ensure that you are in compliance with all the regulations associated with your industry. A business license will also protect both your customers and you. If you are ever sued, your business license will keep your personal assets protected.

Sales Permit

What it is: A sales permit or seller's permit, allows you to sell goods or services in compliance with the local tax codes.

Why you need it: If your business involves collecting sales tax on goods and services, you need a sales permit that will allow you to keep track of taxes collected. This record combined with your permit is how your local taxation agency will keep track of your

taxes due.

Health Department Permit

What it is: Issued by your local permitting

agency, a health department permit is

essential for any business that could impact

public health. A health department permit

indicates that your business complies with

all applicable sanitation and safety laws.

Why you need it: Restaurants and

bakeries sell consumable goods, so a health

department permit is important to have. In

some states, only newly constructed

buildings require a health department

permit. Others require a health department

permit regardless of the status of the

building. Check with your local health department for specific requirements.

Fire Department Permit

What it is: A fire department permit may be required for your brick-and-mortar bakery to demonstrate that you are in compliance with local fire codes.

Why you need it: Bakery equipment like stoves, ovens, and electrical appliances could pose fire hazards if improperly used or maintained. A fire department permit shows that your business is following safety protocols that prevent fire hazards and protect life and property.

Sign Permit

What it is: A sign permit allows you to legally affix permanent or semi-permanent signage to the building's exterior.

Why you need it: Depending on your bakery's location, a sign permit may be required to maintain the standards of surrounding businesses. For example, your city may require that signs be a certain size and there may be rules about what can be written on your sign, brightness, and other factors.

Alcohol License

What it is: Sometimes called a liquor license, alcoholic beverage license, or a liquor permit (depending on your state), an alcohol license allows you to legally serve food and beverages that contain alcohol. In many states, there are different licenses depending on what type of alcohol you offer. For example, in Florida, there are separate licenses for beer and wine vs. hard liquor like vodka, bourbon, or cognac.

Why you might need it: As a baker if you infuse your goods with alcohol, you will likely not need a liquor license. Alcohol generally evaporates in baked goods like rum-infused pound cake. However, if you typically make liquor-themed cakes that include real, unopened bottles of alcohol, this could be considered 'selling liquor to

the public. '

Expect the Unexpected

By now, you should know that my experience was no cakewalk (and yours probably won't be either)! In fact, it got to the point where I almost hated the idea of cake or getting myself into opening the bakery.

Days turned into weeks and what seemed like a pretty simple renovation turned into a complete nightmare! As I told you earlier, I had a few hang-ups with my contractor, but I finally thought we were getting on the right track once the permits were finally obtained. He managed to get the place in somewhat better shape and began to install the plumbing. Since the building had previously been used as a tanning salon, there was no standard plumbing for all of the equipment I would need. The concrete floor had to be torn out and a new one poured after the lines were in place, costing additional money and time.

"Ideally, you want to get everything going so that you can open your bakery and start to recoup some of the money you've invested."

Installing new plumbing took almost a month to complete and added an additional $1k to my renovation budget. All those home renovation shows started to make sense to me now when I would see them going over budget! I became very irritated by the 4th month into construction. This project was not supposed to take this long, and I was constantly having to fork out more money.

Ideally, you want to get everything going so that you can open your bakery and start to recoup some of the money you've invested. When you are at certain points in your renovation, you will have to schedule a walk-through inspection with the city to do a to review the work that has been done. This is where things began to go left!

"I had to continue to adjust my vision to fit my budget and learn to expect the unexpected."

The inspector always gave me a hard time. Every time he came in, he was either late, rude, or found something new to be done or to be corrected! I grew so irritated with him and the time the contractor was taking. One day I came in and there was no progress being made. I called up the contractor and completely lost it! We were now 6 months in, and I had already failed the city inspection four times! The contractor basically told me that I work around his time. I fired him during that phone call in the heat of the argument and demanded that the money that I had put up be refunded for what wasn't completed.

At this point, I am 6 months into a renovation project, I've already signed a 3-year lease agreement, and there's no way I could back out. I started searching

everywhere for anyone who could help me finish everything and not break the bank. I finally found Don! He was a fast talker, but his work spoke volumes, and most importantly: he was cheap!

Don and his buddy worked together, and we came up with a written agreement on a bakery box that was literally our new contract. They worked day and night to help bring the place to the point that I could open! The thing about renovations is, you think you have it all planned out, but things always change on the spot and you have to either adjust to the change or let it weigh you down. I had to continue to adjust my vision

to fit my budget and learn to expect the unexpected.

Chapter 4: Purchasing Equipment

Once the building was actually in what I would call usable order, I had to get equipment. This is where you can literally eat your entire budget up if you don't purchase smart! Of course, you want the finest of equipment and all the new shiny toys, but restaurant equipment is very expensive, and I am a bargain shopper! Even when I buy clothes, I go straight to the clearance rack first. This was no different!

I searched the classifieds and online ads to find used equipment and was able to save thousands! You can also check out companies that rent equipment. This can get costly, but if you need to start with something and build revenue then this may be an ideal way to go. There are also restaurant auctions, wholesale equipment stores, liquidation sales, and so many other places you can find gently used or like-new equipment for a fraction of the cost. Most likely, the bulk of your budget will be reserved for equipment, so also keep in mind that you want to purchase good working equipment – especially your oven!

My oven was the biggest piece of equipment that I lucked up on getting. There was a major chain restaurant in town and the owner posted an oven for sale on Craigslist. I went to take a look at it and told him that I was opening a bakery nearby. He was so impressed that he cut the price in half for me and I ended up only having to pay $500 for a 6 full tray convection oven! Talk about a blessing!

"Most likely, the bulk of your budget will be reserved for equipment, so also keep in mind that you want to purchase good working equipment – especially your oven!"

Some of the must-have equipment includes:

- [ ] Convection oven
- [ ] Microwave
- [ ] 3-Compartment sink
- [ ] Hand-washing Sinks
- [ ] Mixers
- [ ] Cooler
- [ ] Vent hoods
  (required in some areas)

- [ ] Stove
- [ ] Freezer
- [ ] Racks
- [ ] Display Cooler
- [ ] Work Tables
- [ ] POS System (for payments)

This list is comprised of the essentials that you will need when opening your bakery. Many of these items are also required by your local health department. This brings us to the next section: preparing for the health department!

Getting Ready for Health Department Inspections

Your bakery will require an inspection by the health department before opening as well certain documents that must be turned in prior to your inspection date. Each state's requirements will be different, so check

with your local Health Department for the specific requirements for your area. You've probably been working from home for so long that you believe that you have followed all the correct steps to ensure that you're creating food items in a safe environment. WRONG! Many of the practices we use at home are not permitted in food establishments and can cause you to be shut down or even face hefty fines.

The dreadful thought of getting inspected by your local Health Department can be the most agonizing feeling! I literally felt sick because I was worried if I would pass my first walkthrough. Every health inspector is different and he or she will play a key role in approving your permit!

I had already caught hell with the city while trying to get my final permits from them. The city required that I also have a walkthrough of the space to outline what the plans would be. Then, I had to submit a drawing to the Health Department of what the space would look like (just like the drawing that was submitted to the city).

"The permit journey can be a long and frustrating one, so it's always best to make sure you have all of your documents within the required time frames to ensure the inspection process goes as smoothly as possible."

One thing I caught grief about was having a public restroom. Originally, I didn't plan to even have one because it would be too much of a hassle to reroute the pipes that had already been installed. Luckily, my inspector came and showed me how I could save some money by utilizing the existing restroom in the rear of the building. My inspector did her first walkthrough with me to give me an idea of everything that I needed and what I needed to correct before the final inspection. I found out that this was not a common practice of most health inspectors and her guidance saved me so much time and money!

My inspector was extremely helpful and guided me through the entire process. One of my biggest hang-ups was going back and forth with the city and the

Health Department about the need to have a vent hood system installed. I had been told several times by the Health Department that a hood would not be needed since I would not be frying any food items. My oven also had its own built-in ventilation. I literally had to go as far as reaching out to the manufacturer of the oven to send specifications directly to the city stating that the oven did not require a hood. That entire process resulted in another two-week setback!

The permit journey can be a long and frustrating one, so it's always best to make sure you have all of your

documents within the required time frames to ensure the inspection process goes as smoothly as possible.

Chapter 5: It's Time to Open

Many people never ask a question, they never ask for help, they never try a new thing they never start their business, all because they are afraid of being told no. They let that fear paralyze them and keep them in the same place they've always been. I want you to know that there are far worse things that you can be told aside from no. Sometimes, no just means not right now. It doesn't mean give up. That's exactly how I got here. I didn't accept no for an answer.

Before I ever got a chance to open my doors, I had failed my city inspection a total of 11 times! Ten times, I had to hear 'no', 'not approved'. Ten times, I had to

receive another pink paper saying I had failed or needed to change something or buy something else. Every time I heard 'no', in the moment, I felt like it took something out of me. But after all these years of reflecting on those experiences, hearing 'no' actually built me up. Hearing 'no' so many times gave me opportunities to reinvent and perfect my presentation.

Can you imagine working as hard as you can on something, spending every dollar that you've saved, all to be told 'no?' It was hard, but I didn't let it stop me. I kept showing up for myself. I kept showing up for my business.

When I tell the story to most people, their mouths drop. It's true. Now, don't think being knocked down won't hurt. It does. There were times that I became hopeless that I would ever actually pass. Before I let those feelings take over, I would always remind myself of how far I've come. I would remind myself why I do what I do. Sometimes, I would even cry, but I never stopped pushing forward.

During the 11th inspection, the fire chief told me that this would be the last time. I can still hear the sound of his voice when he spoke. His words hit me in the chest like a ton of bricks. I just knew that he could see my heart beating through my shirt! In my head, it was so loud. I remember wondering if I had turned the air on because it seemed to get really hot in the room really fast. I had a million thoughts running through my mind, but I had to take a deep breath and remind myself that my life wasn't in my own hands. It wasn't in the fire chief's hands either.

Now, if you're not religious, it's okay. These next few lines might not be for you. Since I am, I'm going to take this moment to tell you what God has for you, is for you. He won't bring you to anything that he won't bring you through. You can think about it in terms of the universe or any other entity, but my testimony honors what I believe. God brought me to this moment like he'd brought me through before and I had to have faith.

The fire chief and the city inspector walked through. They looked up and down. They opened doors and drawers. Finally, they made their way back to the door where I was waiting to hear my fate. The city inspector looked at me and told me I had passed! I don't even think I actually processed what he said at that moment, but I literally burst into tears.

You see, I could have given up after the first 'no'. I could have given up after the third, fourth, or fifth 'no', but I stayed the course. This message might not be for you but pay attention anyway because you may be able to deliver it to someone else who is experiencing this. It doesn't matter how many times you get knocked down. What matters most is how many times you get up!

So, if you have been going through a season where you're hearing a lot of no's, just know that your 'yes' is on the way. It's always darkest just before dawn, and no matter what the sun always rises.

Writing this book has brought back so many memories and I'm feeling all the same emotions that I felt when I was going through all of these ups and downs. It has also reminded me of how grateful I am for absolutely every one of the experiences that I have had. In every instance, I learned something. I became better. I became stronger. I carried this thing for 9 months. I nurtured it and saw it grow. Even after all of the disappointments and setbacks, I continued to build. When it was time, I felt it. Everything aligned. After 9 months of hearing no, and thousands of dollars lost, I had finally given birth to my baby! It was finally time to prepare to open.

Menu Planning

Before you go out planning your big grand opening, you need to ensure you are ready for the opening and the rush that's about to come! Let's talk about

planning your menu. This was the fun part for me! I had been baking out of my apartment for years, so in that time, I had a chance to play around with flavors and determine what I wanted to offer. I knew that I wanted to have a retail section that offered different treat items daily. I had to be sure to build a menu that would draw in customers and set me apart but not overwhelm me every day.

There are several websites out there that you can use to create your menu template. I would also suggest building a recipe book and laminating the pages. This way, if you are not there, anyone can follow the instructions to achieve the same outcome each time. An important thing to remember is to keep the menu realistic! Although you may feel like you have superpowers, in reality ,you have to be mindful that you can't do it all. When you first get started, you will be excited and want to offer everything you've been dreaming of or have bookmarked on social media. This is a huge mistake!

You have to remember that in some cases if you do not hire staff, you will be doing a lot of this alone. Start off with a limited flavor menu and gradually introduce new flavors to introduce customers to a new flavor palate. Keeping your initial menu limited to a few flavors will also help you with marketing ideas like flavor of the week or month.

You may opt to do an old-fashioned chalkboard display menu or step it up a notch and spend the extra money to have a digital menu, which in my opinion, is a great idea when it comes to ease of customization. Digital menus have a variety of templates that allow you to just input everything and it will automatically format everything in a menu style for you. There are web-based programs like [Canva](#) & [Poster My Wall](#) that make this process very easy.

Recruiting and Hiring

Once you get your menu created, it's time to ensure

you have recipes for everything that you plan to offer. If you hire an assistant or baker, you will want to make sure they create everything the way you would if you were doing it. I know you're thinking, 'No! I

can't let other people know my Nana's prized recipes! '

This is why an NDA or Non-Disclosure Agreement is key. The NDA outlines what information, trade secrets, and products can't be shared outside of your business. A Non-Compete Clause in the new hire packet will also ensure that if an employee separates from your bakery, they cannot do certain things. This is so important if you have staff who try to take special techniques or recipes you've created and go out and try to monetize them for themselves. It is common for bakeries to include a Non-Compete Clause that states the employee can't work within so many miles of their establishment or even work outside of their business for a certain point of time after employment.

This brings me to hiring employees. I literally went through 22 employees in the 3 years I was open! Let's be honest, a lot of people are lazy and lack work ethic in today's society! In a service-based business, customer service is so important. A rude employee can break your business and word of mouth travels fast!

"There is nothing worse than hiring someone and seeing that everything they said during the interview and on their resume was a complete lie!"

Be sure you are looking at potential employees who have the necessary skills to make your job easier. There is nothing worse than hiring someone and seeing that everything they said during the interview and on their resume was a complete lie! Have all decorators or bakers complete a skills test. Decorators should at least know the basics of icing a cake, writing, basic buttercream and fondant techniques, and any other techniques that you may require in your business. It took me a while, but I eventually created an amazing team that had a baker, an assistant decorator, a chocolatier, and a prep person to handle the many tasks that came up around the bakery.

You may not need this many people starting out. My bakery was located in a high traffic area and because of social media, I had developed a pretty good reputation and customer base. Use employment sites to help in your search like Indeed or Craigslist and follow a recruiting checklist to streamline the process.

Once you have gotten the menu and staff out the way, make sure you have a meeting with your accountant or financial advisor to ensure you have everything in order for your bakery opening. You will need a sales tax license to charge sales tax and sell goods. Out of everything you need to successfully open a bakery, I feel that an accountant is the absolute most important person in your business. Hiring a reputable accountant can help you avoid so many headaches and potential fines later on!

Let me tell you a little story. When I first set out to open a bakery, I told you had I had no real business knowledge or any idea what I was doing. I learned pretty much everything by reading information online and asking questions. One area in which I was truly clueless about was the financial side of things. I knew I made pretty good money, but I was clueless about managing it or taking care of the business. My accountant Tonia was a Godsend!

I was one year into the business when I realized that I never paid any sales taxes to the state. Here I was making all this money and owed the state! When I got introduced to Tonia, I was in a pretty bad space with taxes. I owed over $30k and was still racking up a balance! I was not keeping up with receipts at all. I was just making purchases with no real records of anything. Tonia came in and did a complete audit of everything and got me set up on a payment plan to get me on track with the state. Like any business, you will have great months and you will have some slow periods. Well, despite my accountant's efforts, I got

behind on the payment plan and pushed my business further into tax debt. I was getting letters every other week of what I owed and the associated consequences, but I pretty much just ignored them. Being young and dumb!

One Friday afternoon, I was in the middle of completing two wedding cake orders that were due that weekend when the sheriff and two tax officers walked into the bakery and told me that I had to pay $10,000 on the spot or I would need to shut the business down! They confiscated everything I had in the cash drawer and in my on-site safe to go towards the debt. I was so confused and hurt and just mad at myself for letting it get to this point.

The tax officer was really nice and offered her assistance on what I needed to do going forward. I was allowed to finish working on the orders I had, but I had to close for business until the debt was fully paid. I sat up all night crying and beating myself up about how I let myself and my employees down.

"Hiring a reputable accountant can help you avoid so many headaches and potential fines later on! "

The next day, I had the first wedding to complete. I gathered myself and pulled everything together for it. When I arrived at the wedding guess who was there during the set up? The tax officer! She was the florist for the wedding. I was so embarrassed and truly feeling defeated. She came over and looked at the cake once I had it all set up and told me how amazing it was and how I truly had an amazing gift. I dropped my head and said to myself, "Had, but that's over now."

She looked at me straight in the eye and told me to hold my head up. She said she was going to give me some advice off the record. The business I had, JustKaking, LLC was tied to the tax debt that I owed to the state. I didn't understand what she was saying right off. She broke it down a little more and said, "What happens when you start a new business?" I said, "You get a name and all the other legal stuff that goes along with it." Then it hit me! Start a new business! She looked at me and smiled. The key to me keeping my bakery was as simple as changing the name and all legal documents to go with the new name! I called my accountant as soon as I got in the car and she explained all that needed to be done. On that following Tuesday, I re-opened under the new name, Cakes by Kake King, LLC.

Chapter 6: You Can Do It!

At the beginning of this book, I emphasized how important it is to stick with it, no matter how hard things get. The key to your success is consistency so you must remember why you started in the first place!

At the beginning of this book, I emphasized how important it is to stick with it, no matter how hard things get. The key to your success is consistency, so you must remember why you started in the first place! Your 'why' is your purpose for doing what you're doing. It is the driver deep down inside you that keeps you putting one foot in front of the other on even the hardest days. I told you at the beginning of this book about how I started baking. It was an outlet for me. Baking brought me joy during one of the most depressing seasons of my life. It was my silver lining. My glimmer of hope. Baking helped me feel alive again when I felt I had nothing to live for.

As I became better in the kitchen, I was becoming a better person inside. I was healing. I was showing up for myself in a way that I hadn't in the past and the result of that was not only that I was happier and healthier, but I got really good at baking. Actually, I became great at it! The more I work on myself, the more that translates to my craft. Just like the perfect layer of buttercream, you have to gently keep smoothing out the imperfections.

Now, just because you know your why and you have something that is pushing you from the inside that doesn't mean that things don't get hard, or that you won't go through moments or even seasons where you feel tired and discouraged. What it means is that you have something that keeps you grounded. When those storms come, your why will keep you anchored within yourself and your business. So, as you go about your journey, no matter where you are in that process, always remind yourself why you're doing what you're doing. It may be financial freedom. It may be a creative outlet. It may be to support your family or buy a house. You may be following a lifelong dream. No matter what it is, write it down right here. Yes, in this book. Yes, on this page. It's yours! You bought it! It can be in pencil, pen, or crayon. Just grab whatever is handy and write down your 'why'. That way, when you pick up this book again and flip through these pages, you'll pause on this page and be reminded of why you started and what or who you're working for. That moment of realization will bring a sense of gratitude and that little mindful moment may be all you need to continue to keep pushing through even the toughest circumstances.

My Why

_____

_____

_____

_____

_____

I know you chose to read this book because you likely needed help figuring out what it really takes to go from a home baker to having your very own bakery location. You may have even chosen to read this book because you wanted to know my story or simply support my journey. Either way, I want you to always refocus your attention on yourself and honor your why.

As I was writing this book, I watched a friend go through a difficult moment in their business. As that person weathered what I perceived was a storm, they kept affirming why it was so important to correct the issue. It wasn't about the business. It wasn't about the product or service. It was about the why behind all of that. So, the urgency to get the problem fixed was driven completely by their why. It was extremely moving to see their passion. That moment reminded me of my 'why'.

So, if you haven't already, take some time to think that out and use the space designated in this book or any space that you choose and write down your 'why'. It's something that you will come back to again and again. Your why is an essential component of your business and should be a part of every business plan and at the heart of every decision that you make. It will help you stick with it, especially when times get hard.

I wrote this book, because back when I first started baking, I didn't have a resource like this. There wasn't a publication that I found that truly guided me. I learned a lot of things online and through trial and error. There were many times where I was frustrated. There were times where I felt I was wasting time, and there were times where I felt I was wasting money and materials because I wasn't getting the results that I wanted, or it was taking me too much time to get it right. So, I wrote this book and created the companion workbook – not as a step-by-step guide, because each journey is different – but as a resource to lean on and glean from when you get stuck. It is my hope that these materials will potentially save you years of frustration and lead to better outcomes for you.

Going from your home to a brick-and-mortar location can be overwhelming. There's so much to remember and so many steps to take! But don't get discouraged. Every baker had to start somewhere and experience setbacks along the way – even me! Mistakes are inevitable, but they are a necessary part of the process. You will learn as you go and that's okay. The good thing is you have this book to help you along your journey of opening your very own bakery.

One thing I will caution here is to be careful of looking too closely into what others in the industry or those around you are doing. You are one of a kind. There is no one in this world like you. You are unique and special and so is everything you create. It is perfectly fine to be inspired by another person or their work.

You may see a technique and think immediately to yourself how you can use it in your business, or how you can take it a step further and create something totally different.

Don't get too caught up in what other people are doing. Focus on you. Focus on your why, and that is where you will find the most joy – and likely make the most money – because you will be tapping into something that no one else has access to but you.

As you continue this journey and have a desire to do more, go further, and be better, know that you will come into contact with all kinds of information and advice. You can type a question into a search bar, and it will return hundreds, even thousands of potential answers. You can ask a question on social media and will receive tons of comments, each expressing an individual's idea or something that reflects what they would do or how they would respond to whatever the prompt is. But even in those answers, the one you choose will still need to be tailored to you.

So, consume everything. Ask all the questions that you feel are necessary. Take the information that you find and use what you need in the way that you need it and leave the rest. Don't get bogged down trying to follow the steps of another person's journey. Even in the bonus section of this book, I tell you to tweak the recipes and make them your own. Again, this is about you and your 'why'. As long as you stay true to that, I have no doubt that you will reach all of your goals and live out your dreams.

I'm sure you've gathered by reading this, that I pour my heart and soul into everything I do, and this book is no different. All I ask is that you do the same as you go about opening your storefront. Take things one step at a time, but take your steps. Take good notes but use them in a way that is applicable to you and what you do. Set smart goals for yourself and honor your progress towards them. Focus on milestones. For example, if one of your goals on your journey to opening your own storefront is to obtain a building permit, celebrate yourself when you apply for it. You've taken a critical step to obtain the permit just by completing the application and paying the necessary fees. If you never completed the application, you'd never be awaiting approval or be granted the permit.

So, check even the smallest things off your list as you begin to take steps to open your location. Celebrate every win no matter how big or small, because, without those little wins along the way, you'd never be in competition for a grand prize. When things go well, take note of what you did to get there and look for ways to make it even better. When things don't go as planned, take a moment to see where you went wrong, then recommit to your vision.

Remember, you are bringing your personal brand from your home environment to the public, so you want to present your best self at all times. Operating in excellence at all times will help build your brand and solidify your place as a true professional. While your brand is a key component of you, understand that while you are growing and building and trying new things, that not everyone will like everything that you produce. Take the feedback in its entirety without judgment. Use what is applicable to you in the ways that you can and leave the rest. Most importantly, remember your 'why' and stick with it no matter what.

Chapter 7: Bonuses

You know I wouldn't write this book and not include
Some of the recipes that have taken my business to
unimaginable levels. I'm going to share with you some
of my tried-and-true recipes. Feel free to tweak them
and make them your own.

But before I release you to your kitchens to do what
you do best, I want you to know that I am proud of
you. I don't have to know your story to know that you

have one. I know you've been through something. You've overcome something. You've lost something. You've endured something. And you've survived it all. You are still here. You are still baking, and I'm proud of you. You can get 100 no's, but the right yes at the right time can change the trajectory of your entire life. You are unique. You are special, and you matter.

If you don't take anything else from this book, take that message with you and share it with someone else. Thank you for being on this journey with me. Now, let's get in the kitchen and bake something beautiful.

King's No Fail Cake Recipe

2 Boxes Cake Mix (works with any flavor) 2 Cups Pillsbury All Purpose Flour

1 Cup Sugar

1 Cup Oil

1 Cup Buttermilk

2 Cups Water

6 Eggs

Flavoring (use as desired)

Directions:

1. Mix all wet ingredients first.
2. Add in dry ingredients.
3. *Oven Temp: 340°
4. For cakes: bake 40-45 min.
5. For cupcakes: bake 12-15 Minutes.

My Big Mama's Favorite Pound Cake!

Cream Cheese Pound Cake

1 1/2 cup butter, softened

1 8 oz. pkg. cream cheese 3 cups sugar

6 eggs

3 cups All-Purpose Flour 1/8 tsp salt

1 Tbsp vanilla extract

1 Tbsp almond extract

Directions:

1. Beat the butter and cream cheese at medium speed with electric mixer until creamy. Gradually add sugar, beating until light and fluffy.
2. Add eggs, 1 at a time, beating just until blended after addition.
3. Combine flour and salt; gradually add to butter mixture, beating on low speed just until blended. Stir in vanilla.
4. Spoon batter into a greased and floured 10-inch tube pan.

5. *Bake at 300° for 1 hour and 45 minutes or until wooden pick inserted in center comes out clean. Cool in pan on wire rack 15 minutes. Remove from pan and let cool completely on wire rack.

*Helpful Hint: Don't preheat the oven

Buttercream Recipe

4 Sticks Unsalted Butter

1 Cup Shortening (allows the buttercream to crust and hold up in high temperature environments) 6 - 8 Cups Confectioners' Sugar

1/4 Cup Heavy Whipping Cream

Add Flavoring or Coffee Creamer

Directions:

1. Whip butter one stick at a time until creamy add shortening.
2. Add in powdered sugar one cup at a time.

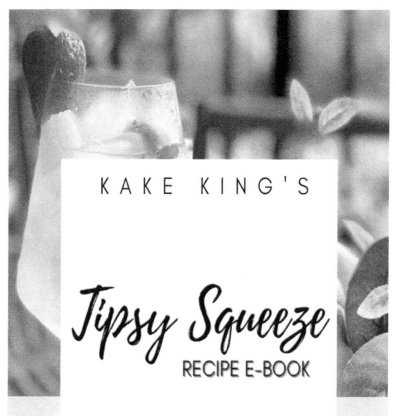

KAKE KING'S

Tipsy Squeeze

RECIPE E-BOOK

· ·

WWW.KAKEKING.COM

IT'S LEMONADE WITH A
LITTLE SOMETHING
EXTRA!

COPYRIGHT DISCLAIMER

ABOUT THE BOOK

Drink Up!

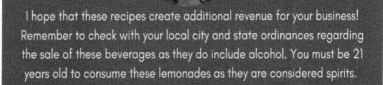

I hope that these recipes create additional revenue for your business! Remember to check with your local city and state ordinances regarding the sale of these beverages as they do include alcohol. You must be 21 years old to consume these lemonades as they are considered spirits.

Please drink responsibly!

Kake King

 @iamkakeking   iamkakeking

WWW.KAKEKING.COM

Table of Contents

Master Recipe

INGREDIENTS

1 Gallon (16 Cups) Water
4 Cups Sugar
2 Cups Country Time Lemonade Mix
5 Cups Pineapple Juice

INSTRUCTIONS

- Mix all ingredients in a large pitcher using warm water so that the sugar dissolves easier.
- Allow to chill or serve over ice

To add flavor variations to the base, you can use flavor syrups such as Strawberry, Peach, Mango, etc.

Lemon Berry
Rita

Lemon Berry Rita

INGREDIENTS

12oz Bottle Recipe
**Add 2oz additional
alcohol
per bottle for 16oz bottles.

8oz Lemonade Base
2oz Hennessy
1oz Grand Marnier
1oz Strawberry Daiquiri Mix

WWW.KAKEKING.COM

Hot Girl Summer
Tipsy Squeeze
Hot Girl Summer
INFUSED LEMONADE
Tipsy Squeeze
Hot Girl Summer
INFUSED LEMONADE

Hot Girl Summer

INGREDIENTS

12oz Bottle Recipe
**Add 2oz additional alcohol
per bottle for 16oz bottles.

6oz Lemonade Base
2oz Strawberry Lemondade
Vodka
2oz Bacardi Rum
2oz Strawberry Daiquiri Mix

WWW.KAKEKING.COM

Island

Breeze

Island Breeze

INGREDIENTS

12oz Bottle Recipe
**Add 2oz additional
alcohol
per bottle for 16oz bottles.

7oz Lemonade Base
2oz Pineapple Ciroc
2oz Malibu Rum
1oz Vodka

WWW.KAKEKING.COM

Strawberry Pineapple Moscato

Tipsy

Strawberry Pineapple Moscato

INGREDIENTS

12oz Bottle Recipe
**Add 2oz additional alcohol
per bottle for 16oz bottles.

5oz Lemonade Base
4oz Moscato Wine
2oz Vodka
1oz Strawberry Daiquiri Mix

NOTES

You may use flavored vodka or flavored wine to add more flavor! You may also change the flavor syrup and wine flavor to change the flavor.

Green Apple
Moscato

Green Apple Moscato

INGREDIENTS

12oz Bottle Recipe
**Add 2oz additional
alcohol
per bottle for 16oz bottles.

5oz Lemonade Base
4oz Green Apple Moscato
Wine
2oz Vodka
1oz Apple Pucker

Thank You!

WANT TO LEARN MORE?

If you need a more hands on approach, sign up for the virtual class!

Sign Up Now

WWW.KAKEKING.COM

About the Author

A Mississippi native, Jeromie "Kake King" Jones has over 15 years of baking experience. As a two-time Food Network competitor, Jeromie has always strived to be among the best cake artists in the world. His artistic ability combined with his business savvy has also helped him become a mentor to fellow bakers and business owners all over the world.